BITCOIN

Complete Guide to Mastering Bitcoin Mining, Trading, and Investing

MATT COHEN

Copyright © 2017 Matt Cohen - All rights reserved.

In no way is it legal to reproduce, duplicate, or transmit any part of this document in either electronic means or in printed format. recording of this publication is strictly prohibited and any storage of this document is not allowed unless with written permission from the publisher. all rights reserved. The information provided herein is stated to be truthful and consistent, in that any liability, in terms of inattention or otherwise, by any usage or abuse of any policies, processes, or directions contained within is the solitary and utter responsibility of the recipient reader. under no circumstances will any legal responsibility or blame be held against the publisher for any reparation, damages, or monetary loss due to the information herein, either directly or indirectly. Respective authors own all copyrights not held by the publisher. The information herein is offered for informational purposes solely, and is universal as so. the presentation of the information is without contract or any type of guarantee assurance. The trademarks that are used are without any consent, and the publication of the trademark is without permission or backing by the trademark owner. all trademarks and brands within this book are for clarifying purposes only and are the owned by the owners themselves, not affiliated with this document. The author wishes to thank the following people for the images of this book: bitcoin.com, bitcoincharts.com, KryptoNatasha, ngzhang, Alan Reiner (GNU Affero General Public License), Blockchain.info, Stickac. Unless specified differently, all the images are released under Creative Commons CC-BY-SA License.

TABLE OF CONTENTS

Free Bonus: 5 Proven And Legitimate Ways To Earn Money From Your Computer	7
Introduction	9
Chapter 1: Intro to Bitcoin	11
Chapter 2: Understanding Blockchains and Transactions	29
Chapter 3: Mining for Profit	35
Chapter 4: Trading for Profit	49
Chapter 5: Investing in Bitcoin	53
Chapter 6: Bitcoin Wallets and Securing Your Coin	59
Conclusion	69

BITCOIN

MATT COHEN

FREE BONUS
MAKE MONEY ONLINE - 5 PROVEN AND LEGITIMATE WAYS TO EARN MONEY FROM YOUR COMPUTER

The majority of people thinks earning an income through the internet is just a dream, or alternatively some sort of scam. However, there are many legitimate ways to earn money from your computer.

In this short guide you're about to discover 5 proven ways you can follow to actually start making money online, for real. Each one comes with a rating based on 3 factors:

- How quick can you actually earn your first dollar? (5 stars = really quick)
- Is it easy for a beginner with little to no previous experience? (5 stars = really easy)
- Is it cheap to start or does it require a high investment? (5 stars = really cheap or free)

Go to **www.eepurl.com/c5Ybb1** to download the free guide.

MATT COHEN

INTRODUCTION

Congratulations on downloading this book and thank you for doing so. The world of Bitcoin can initially be intimidating and hard to completely comprehend. With this book, you have a personal guide arming you with the tools you'll need and leading you through the different challenges presented by Bitcoin mining, trading, and investing.

The following chapters will provide a thorough understanding of Bitcoin mining, trading, and investing for profit. Discussed in-depth includes crucial information and base principles regarding Bitcoin and its related systems, how to go about Bitcoin mining for profit, wise cryptocurrency investing practices, the importance of carefully choosing and securing Bitcoin wallets as well as other currency storage methods (paper wallets, cold storage, etc.), information regarding blockchain technology and transactions, and all of the other information you'll need to make the most out of Bitcoin.

Several resources are provided here, including profit calculators specific to Bitcoin mining, reliable and authentic Bitcoin exchanges, informative examples of trusted mining software and hardware, where to go to buy, sell, and exchange coins, reliable digital wallet apps, and many more tools to give you an upper hand in the world of Bitcoin.

Whether you're a beginner in the world of digital currency or you're a more seasoned Bitcoin miner, the content of this book aims to provide you with the complete information and extensive know-how you need to understand Bitcoin and start making a valuable profit using unique technological and investing savvy.

There are plenty of books on this subject on the market, thanks again for choosing this one. Every effort was made to ensure it is full of as much useful information as possible, please enjoy!

CHAPTER 1
INTRO TO BITCOIN

Bitcoin (commonly denoted as either BTC or XTC) is a relatively new, rapidly growing, and open-source entirely virtual currency (or, cryptocurrency) system powered by its users. Part of its appeal is a decentralized nature, a lack of a middleman or a primary authority including that of a government or bank. This places the power directly into the hands of its users, Other appealing features are Bitcoin's simplicity in use, instantaneous payments, less expensive transaction system compared to other methods and the resulting freedom from transaction fees for users, somewhat anonymous payments (usernames are never revealed, only public digital wallet IDs and anonymity is further protected when users only use each Bitcoin address once), refreshing ease of international payments, and lack of need of a bank account to receive payments. Other cryptocurrencies and digital goods pose the problem of double spending, but this problem is answered by Bitcoin's unique blockchain system and peer-to-peer (P2P) network. Since its recent surge in popularity, many more people have grown curious about Bitcoin and how to utilize it for investment and profit, as well as acknowledging its possibility and potential as the future of a modern currency.

New Bitcoins are generated by voluntary user computer

power. When users engage in what is called mining, where transactions are verified by blocks being solved (covered more thoroughly in later chapters), hashes are created and a small compensation or fee is paid to the miner. Each time 210,000 new blocks are added to the blockchain, generally every four years in accordance with current trends, the feel is halved. The fee will keep being halved until it reaches zero and exactly 21 million Bitcoins are in circulation.

Bitcoin symbol, a capital letter B with two falling strokes at the top and bottom.

Renowned for its innovation in fraud control, cost efficiency, transparent payment ledger system, and global accessibility, Bitcoin transcends simply sending money back and forth. Some of its current common uses include donations, paying tips, micropayments such as those used to pay online services by the second, and crowdfunding campaigns such as those seen on Kickstarter. A list of verified and well-established foundations that accept Bitcoin donations can be found here: *https://en.Bitcoin.it/wiki/Donation-accepting_organizations_and_projects.* These include Blendernation, a project for the popular free 3D art modeling tool Blender, and LibreOffice, free open-source word software, as well as the Human Rights Foundation and Mozilla Foundation. There is even a church on the list, the Shoreline Unitarian Universalist Church. Universities are even jumping on board, as the University of Nicosia now accepts Bitcoins as a valid tuition payment.

Other uses for the service are constantly being contemplated and eventually implemented, and what Bitcoin is not yet being used for is perhaps the most exciting. Bitcoins can even be used to purchase virtual gift cards on popular company website Gyft.

Drawbacks to Bitcoin currently include the lack of universal acceptance of the currency, the constantly shifting value, and the fact that Bitcoin is still in beta and actively being developed. Most Bitcoin companies do not offer insurance and many features are still incomplete. Taxes and tax liability are still included within certain jurisdictions, according to the user's area, and users should be diligent in knowing their location's specific guidelines for the digital currency.

Getting started with the basic aspects of Bitcoin, while seemingly overwhelming, is a relatively simple process once sufficient research has been done.

A user begins by carefully choosing and downloading a digital wallet for their Bitcoins to be stored in. This is a delicate process as not all digital wallets are created with equal security or the same features, and so research must be conducted in order to make a wise, informed decision. Chapter six of this book discusses digital (and non-digital) wallet options and features in detail.

Next, the user will add Bitcoins to their wallet using that wallet's address. Bitcoins can be purchased from a variety of places. The main website's buying page (found here: *https://buy.Bitcoin.com/*), however, is the first place many users start.

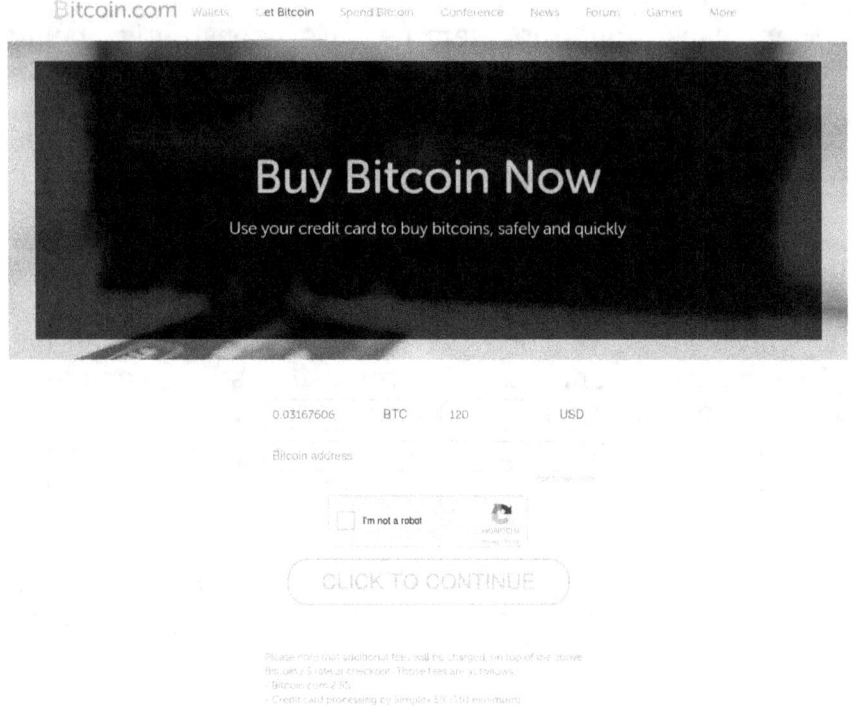

A screenshot of the main website's buying page

When the user is ready to receive Bitcoin, they share their public address with the future sender. When the user is ready to send Bitcoin, they enter the future receiver's public address into a Send box in their digital wallet. When the amount and receiver address are confirmed, they are sent.

The History of Bitcoin. While Bitcoin is not the first cryptocurrency, it is the most successful. In 2007, a paper called *Bitcoin: A Peer-to-Peer Electronic Cash System* was published to a mailing list under the author name Satoshi Nakamoto. The paper described an electronic transaction system that would, in the fall of 2008, become Bitcoin. The first block of Bitcoins, the genesis block, was mined by Nakamoto himself. This block was said to yield 50 Bitcoins, while today one block yields approximately 12.5 Bitcoins, thus increasing the demands and difficulty of Bitcoin mining. The first receiver of a Bitcoin transaction and long-time supporter and contributor was Hal Finney, for 100 Bitcoins. Nick Szabo – the creator of Bitcoin's predecessor, Bit Gold – was another early supporter.

"Nakamoto" is believed to have mined one million Bitcoins before ceasing all involvement with the Bitcoin project. There are speculations that Nakamoto was, in fact, several people under one name, but the true identity of Bitcoin's creator remains a much-discussed mystery. Developer Gavin Andersen took over as lead developer at Bitcoin's face community, the Bitcoin Foundation.

As Bitcoin's popularity began to grow, more businesses and vendors began to accept the cryptocurrency, and as a result, the value of the coin began to expand. The first physical Bitcoin transaction to take place was when an individual paid 10,000 Bitcoins to order pizza. One of the early businesses to accept Bitcoin was popular computer dealer Dell and, naturally, Microsoft. A current list of businesses who accept Bitcoins as payment can be found here: *http://spendBitcoins.com/places/*. In late 2009, the value of Bitcoin was established at 1,309 Bitcoins for $1, and Bitcoin 0.2 was publicly released. Mining difficulty increased for the first time. In 2010, the Bitcoin market cap hit above one million dollars. In five years' time, one Bitcoin's worth rocketed from $0 to $1,000.

In 2011, physical Bitcoins were created by a company in the United States. However, the U.S. Treasury did not approve when they discovered the company's actions. They have since closed down. Alderney was the first jurisdiction to begin and sustain the creation of physical Bitcoins and reportedly still does today.

It has not been exclusive the United States. The Bitcoin donation given to Jet Li's charity sparked an interest of the currency in China. The first Bitcoin ATM was established in Vancouver, Canada. When Argentina's currency saw considerable inflation, Bitcoin rocketed in popularity in the country.

Bitcoin has also not been exclusive to wholesome activities. Ross Ulbricht – under the username Dread Pirate Roberts – was arrested for operating the Silk Road website in 2013. The site made a good deal of money in running a Bitcoin exchange geared towards illegal activities, such as the sale of drugs, prostitution, and hitman services. Besides drugs and hitmen, Bitcoins are also capable of being used to buy pizza, cars, plane tickets, and several other goods and services, depending on the specific business and its location.

Despite constant declarations of "the death of Bitcoin," the numbers have continued a steady climb over the last several years and Bitcoin has been gaining lots of media attention. Today, there are 20,000 computers acting as nodes, powered by Bitcoin miners. One Bitcoin is now worth approximately $4,000 and this value is still increasing over time. This is despite its chaotic changes, such as dropping in value by $200 in just one day and raising again the next. 2140 is estimated to be the year the last Bitcoin will be mined, but this is ultimately only an educated guess.

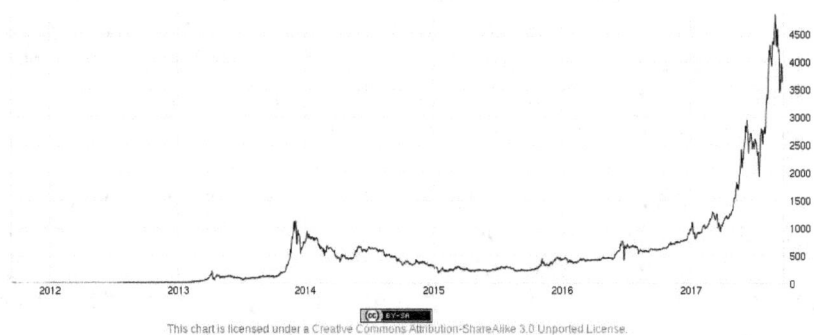

**Currency conversion chart
for Bitcoin to US Dollar (2011 - 2017)**

Addresses. Before users can send or receive Bitcoins, they need to first obtain a digital address. Addresses are obtained upon download of the Bitcoin client or of a digital or online wallet. Bitcoin Core is the most popular client choice for users who have the free disk space to spare, while slightly more compact alternatives are available such as BLANK. Previously, popular clients Multibit and Multibit HD praised for their compactness, well-established reputations, and strong security are as of recently no longer in service. Prior Multibit users were encouraged by developers to move their wallets to Electrum due to ease of import between the two applications and Electrum's automatic multiple address pre-generation.

When Bitcoins are sent, cryptographically signed messages are actually being sent and associated with the address of the recipient. The blockchain processes these transactions using non-biased mathematical equations ran by nodes, user computers mining blocks in return for profit. Typos are not a typical issue as Bitcoins cannot be sent to invalid addresses.

Via creating many different addresses and only using each address one time only for purchases, user anonymity can be sufficiently protected. Several addresses can be held within a single wallet, but there are some security advantages to using multiple wallets and storage methods. Users do not need to be online to receive coins but do need to be online to access them. Leaving the Bitcoin client running ensures the best connectivity, flow of the blockchain, and faster transaction speeds.

User information is protected by these addresses. That being said, users do not always know who they are buying or selling from. Fortunately, the Bitcoin and blockchain systems rely on not needing an absolute trust of buyers or sellers, because the network itself takes care of ensuring the security of transactions. Bitcoin transactions cannot be canceled, user information cannot be traced, and anonymity is well protected.

Buying Bitcoin. A new user's first Bitcoin purchase will usually take the longest, and then the process will significantly speed up. Where Bitcoins should be bought depends on the specific needs and goals of the buyer, namely how they would prefer to purchase Bitcoins (with a credit card, cash, etc.) and where they would prefer to go (offline and in-person versus online locations). The limit to how many Bitcoins a new user can purchase is usually initially relatively small and grows as the user proves to be reliable.

Two of the most popular places to purchase Bitcoins online are Coinmama and Coinbase. SpectroCoin is a popular option for users mainly in Europe, while Kraken serves as a popular and well-established place to buy and exchange Bitcoins as well as other cryptocurrencies. For users planning on buying Bitcoins with a debit or credit card, there is an increased chance of fraud as well as typically higher fees involved in the transaction process.

Local Bitcoin ATMs can be found in many areas using Bitcoin ATM maps, such as the Coin ATM Radar found here: *https://coinatmradar.com/*. There are currently approximately 1,560 Bitcoin ATMs in existence. Different models of ATMs can change how they're used to buy or sell Bitcoins. The different machine types are the Genesis1, Lamassu, Satoshi1, Robocoin, Skyhook, BitAccess, General Bytes BATMTwo, and General Bytes BATMThree.

**A two-way Bitcoin ATM in Toronto
that allows users to buy or sell bitcoins with cash.**

Despite some differences in these different models, a general buying process is followed by all ATMs. There may be first a verification step – such as providing a mobile phone number and entering a verification code sent to that phone – and then the user will provide their Bitcoin address for deposit, enter cash, and Bitcoins are deposited into the user's digital wallet upon confirmation. If a user purchases Bitcoins without previously having their own wallet already established, the Satoshi1 and BATMThree systems may print a paper wallet for the user. It is strongly encouraged to move Bitcoins from this receipt to a safer wallet as soon as possible, and paper wallets are not on their own a secure form of storage.

The only purchase methods that provide total anonymity and do not reveal any of the buyer's personal information are cash and cash deposit. Bank transfers, PayPal, debit or credit cards, and other methods may reveal identifying information. Cash exchanges, typically, have no limits, though the limit to how many Bitcoins you can purchase and how much you can spend will vary from seller to seller.

Selling Bitcoin. Users looking to sell their Bitcoins have three primary options; in-person sales, ATM sales, and online selling. Each selling method provides their own set of advantages and disadvantages regarding convenience, security, and timeliness.

In-person selling provides all parties involved with the most privacy and often buyers won't request any personal information from sellers. These sales are typically cash-only and sellers must execute caution when agreeing to meet up with potential buyers. LocalBitcoins is the most popular place to search for potential in-person Bitcoin sale opportunities. Most of these will include cash deposits in exchange for the seller's Bitcoins. The website can be found here: *https://localBitcoins.com/*. Local Bitcoin meetup groups are another option for in-person selling and possess the potential to connect sellers with regular buyers. Meetup groups, however, are not established in all areas. Meetup provides a list of groups for sellers to join, found here: *https://www.meetup.com/topics/Bitcoin/.* Searching for local Facebook groups involved in Bitcoin exchanges is another potential option, often providing more leads than Meetup can when conducted in smaller areas that are less aware of Bitcoin.

In areas where there are Bitcoin ATMs, selling is occasionally an option from directly on the ATM. Many Bitcoin ATMs only offer the option to buy, but the Coin ATM Radar provides information and maps regarding which machines offer both buying and selling. Fees for these ATM exchanges should be carefully observed, as many fees will severely decrease profits and may not be at all worth it.

Online selling is, naturally, probably the most popular and convenient Bitcoin sales method. This method does lack the same level of privacy that is offered by the other two methods. Users can create sell orders on available Bitcoin selling websites. If a buyer accepts the order offer, the buyer receives the seller's bank account information and makes a cash deposit. Popular websites used for selling include Coinbase and Circle Internet Financial *(https://www.circle.com/en/)*, praised for its mobile texting format design.

Legality. Despite any of those individual concerns, Bitcoin is legal in a majority of jurisdictions. Locations where foreign currency is restricted or banned, such as Russia, may pose a concern when using Bitcoin. While rules are still in the process of being established for virtual currencies such as Bitcoin, the Financial Crimes Enforcement Network of the United States Treasury Department has released legal guidance on its classifications regarding online virtual currency activities. In short, Bitcoin *is* a legal activity in most countries.

Concerns surrounding illegal activities being more easily conducted using currencies such as Bitcoin, taking advantage of the system's ease of use and anonymity, are no different than those surrounding cash.

Countries Where Bitcoin is Legal:
- Argentina
- Australia
- Bosnia
- Belgium
- Bulgaria
- Brazil
- Canada
- Colombia
- Chile
- China – it is only legal here for private parties to exchange Bitcoin, not banks, companies, or similar institutions
- Croatia
- Cyprus
- Czech Republic
- Denmark
- Estonia
- Finland
- France
- Germany
- Greece
- Hong Kong
- Iceland
- India
- Indonesia
- Ireland
- Israel – miners and traders here are taxed as businesses
- Japan
- Jordan – discouraged by government, Bitcoins are accepted here by small businesses, but cannot be accepted by banks, financial companies, payment services, or currency exchanges
- Lebanon – discouraged by government, but is

regardless still legal
- Liberland – the Free Republic here actually holds part of its reserves in digital currencies
- Luxembourg
- Malaysia
- Malta – the country's 2017 prime minister has approved a national strategy to promote and encourage Bitcoin and blockchain systems
- Mexico
- Nicaragua
- Nigeria
- Netherlands
- New Zealand
- Norway
- Pakistan – as of 2017, the Federal Board of Revenue is investigating digital currency trade for money laundering and tax evasion
- Philippines
- Poland
- Portugal
- Romania
- Saudi Arabia
- Singapore
- Slovakia
- Slovenia
- Spain – Bitcoin transactions are subject to the same laws here as barter exchanges
- South Africa
- South Korea
- Switzerland
- Sweden
- Taiwan – ATMs dealing in Bitcoins are banned here, but the coins can still be purchased and used at popular convenience stores
- Thailand – previously declared illegal in 2013, now business licenses are required to use or transfer Bitcoins
- Turkey

- United Kingdom
- United States – it is taxed here as a commodity per IRS regulations
- Vietnam
- Zimbabwe

Countries Where Bitcoin is Illegal:
- Bangladesh
- Bolivia
- Ecuador
- Kyrgyzstan
- Russia*

*While Bitcoin use and trading in Russia is not yet technically illegal and is still considered unregulated, it is widely discouraged and generally considered illegal.

Anonymity. Bitcoin transactions do not use users' name, identity, or any identifying personal information. Only the user's public Bitcoin address is visible during transactions. However, the public address reveals how many Bitcoins a user has in their possession and every transaction that user has ever made.

Users might hide their public address or IP address using services such as a VPN. Previously, users implemented the services of popular and well-established Bitmixer.io, but this website is no longer in service due to the owner's change of interests in deciding that Bitcoin's openness was not a mistake and the benefits of this system outweighed the benefits of individuals' privacy. The owner, in their parting note, commented on similar services to their own being used for illegal activity and how, because of this, privacy protection services like this one would all be ruled illegal in the near future.

With the closing of Bitmixer.io, many users speculated law enforcement became involved and demanding the high-profiting service be shut down. Bitmixer.io denied all claims of law enforcement involvement or government pressure and insisted it was simply a change of interests with the best intentions for Bitcoin's future in mind, concerned about the effect illegal dealings would eventually surely have on Bitcoin. However, there is a lot of user speculation that there was much more going on behind the shutdown of the website and services. Currently, there are no well-established alternatives to Bitmixer.io, at least not on the same level of success and user trust.

Hacking and Quantum Computer Concerns. Blockchain technology is anti-fraud in nature in that it becomes more difficult to break into the more users are on the network. Today, Bitcoin's network has a computing power already greater than the world's fastest supercomputers. Taking over this network would prove to be very, very difficult if not virtually impossible. Hacking would be mostly futile anyway as there isn't much to be done once the network is taken over. Hackers cannot, from this network, steal other users' Bitcoin funds, create counterfeit or copy coins, or process false transactions. A hacker can reclaim their recently sent coins or prevent transactions from gaining confirmations. This kind of attack, however, would be extremely costly and would deplete many of the hacker's resources. The costs would far outweigh any incentives to hack the Bitcoin system, and the network would resume normal functions immediately when the attack came to a stop.

While a sufficiently large quantum computer would be capable of disrupting the Bitcoin network, it is very unlikely for this to happen, let alone for it to do much damage, due to the way the Bitcoin system is set up. The top concern for this kind of breach would be against cryptography of public keys. It would take a relatively large quantum computer to perform this kind of breach, but it is a possibility using Shor's Algorithm. However, a quantum computer capable of performing this task against Bitcoin would need approximately 1,500 qubits. The biggest modern-day quantum computer only has less than 10. While it cannot be predicted how soon the kind of technology needed to execute a breach might advance, it is known that – in present day – it is impossible. One company, D-Wave, has made claims to possess a special-purpose quantum computer containing over 1,000 qubits. These claims have not been verified. In addition, a *special-purpose* quantum computer would be incapable of attacking Bitcoin technology.

Who Can Use Bitcoin? The use of Bitcoin is not restricted exclusively to business masterminds and computer geniuses, but rather can be used by practically anyone with the right information and tools at their disposal. Bitcoin mining, investing, and trading can be conducted as either an easy currency transaction system to buy everyday goods and services or as a promising new source of extra supplemental income. Bitcoin developers have stressed that they do not promise anyone investing or mining their coins to become rich, but there is still a variety of potential for a profit to be made.

The number of those using Bitcoin has grown enough that the total value of Bitcoin currency has exceeded 20 billion US dollars since the end of April 2017, and millions of more coins are traded in the network every single day. Popular businesses, stores, salons, and online services including well-known sites such as Reddit, among many others, use Bitcoin. While not every business accepts the currency, its popularity is continually growing.

Bitcoin for Business Owners. Cryptocurrency can be somewhat difficult to understand or embrace for business owners who aren't well versed in technology. What business owners should primarily know about accepting Bitcoin as payment for their goods and services is that it is a relatively simple process. Customers either scan a wallet code or click a button, payment shows up, and that payment is confirmed within an hour. These payments are also final, there are no chargebacks, which greatly reduces the risk of fraud for business owners. Bitcoin also removes all of the complications found in dealing with international currencies, including the fees. In addition to those benefits, accepting Bitcoin payments reaches out to a broader market and provides a sense of impressive modernity to customers. Payments in Bitcoins can be deposited into a banking account immediately and payment processors such as Coinbase (the most trusted payment processor for use in the United States, in addition to being free of fees and easily set up) handle all of the technical processing as well as keeping all sales records, making the exchange user-friendly and low maintenance.

The drawbacks to using payment processors are the same drawbacks found in most technology dealing with finances. Hacking and theft is always a possibility, as well as malicious entities releasing a business' information from the processors should they be compelled to do so.

Exchange Communities. Users can acquire Bitcoins through exchanges, user trading, payment for goods and services, or mining. Receiving payments through Bitcoin is as simple as downloading a Bitcoin wallet program on your computer or mobile device, generating a one-time usage Bitcoin address, sharing this address to the person you want to pay you, and then creating more single-use addresses whenever you need them.

Exchanges allow you to interchange your other currency – such as U.S. dollar, PayPal, credit card, or debit card – for Bitcoins. This is how coins may be transferred between users. A master list of popular participating Bitcoin exchanges can be found on Bitcoin's website, categorized by country, here: *https://Bitcoin.org/en/exchanges.*

To better understand Bitcoin amounts and their most current worth, a unit conversion chart goes as follows:

- 1 BTC = 1 Bitcoin
- 1 Satoshi = 0.00000100 BTC
- 1mBTC = 0.001000000 BTC
- 1 Bitcent (cBTC) = 0.01 BTC
- 1 BTC = 3,592 U.S. Dollars
- 1 BTC = 3,007 Euros

- 1 BTC = 399,067 Japanese Yen

Blockchain Processing. A group of cooperating computers or nodes, operated by the system's users, is used to confirm Bitcoin transactions in the processing stage by entering them into the blockchain system after being agreed upon. These agreements, powered by the user-ran nodes, are based on unbiased mathematical algorithms and strict automatic rules.

This entails allowing users to compete in utilizing their hardware to solve complex mathematical equations and in turn be rewarded with the Bitcoin transaction fees within the block. Each new block is added in this way to a preexisting chain, starting with block 1 or the genesis block. This process enforces a chronological order in the chain and protects network neutrality. Transactions must follow a very rigid set of cryptographic rules in order to be confirmed, and these rules do not allow previous blocks to be altered, replaced, or deleted.

Bitcoin Core is a program designed to determine the authenticity of block transactions. Nodes are only capable of accepting valid transactions to be added to the blockchain. This protects the decentralized element of the blockchain network and Bitcoin. A lack of bias is also presented by the software following all the same mathematical rules to evaluate processing blocks.

As the web begins to evolve and adapt to include Bitcoin and other cryptocurrencies, the everyday consumer will more often begin running into Bitcoin features and machines. Already in several small businesses Bitcoins are accepted as payments and Bitcoin ATMs are present. To further service to the everyday customer, there are discounts available to users shopping with their Bitcoins online. Apps and websites now exist enabling Bitcoin payments to be used on popular online stores and websites, such as Amazon. Purse.io is a website that provides just that capability for Bitcoin users. Here, a user can search for Amazon items and pay for them in Bitcoin at a discount compared to paying in U.S. dollars.

CHAPTER 2
UNDERSTANDING BLOCKCHAINS AND TRANSACTIONS

Blockchains were first made popular and more widely recognized through Bitcoin. The blockchain is a public ledger of every transaction ever made through the Bitcoin client, including those that have sent you coins and those that you have sent elsewhere. Proof of each transaction on the network is permanently and publicly recorded here. Recent transactions are held in "blocks" and archived within the blockchain later, each block representing updates of users' account balances. New blocks are continuously being added to the chain as other blocks are completed.

While an extensive knowledge of blockchains is not necessary to utilize the technology, a basic understanding of the process can be helpful when delving into Bitcoin. The process of making a transaction is relatively simple. When someone requests a transaction, that transaction is sent to a network of computers or nodes, and this network validates the transaction using mathematical algorithms. Once verified, the transaction merges with other transactions to create a new block. This block is permanently added to the blockchain, and the transaction is complete. Payments through this type of transaction take an average of ten minutes to be processed. Digital signatures corresponding to user sending addresses ensure each transaction is protected and cryptography ensures the money being transferred is really there. This system allows nodes to act as administrators of the blockchain and verify each transaction as authentic and secure.

Rather than being singularly edited and passed between parties, blockchain technology allows all involved parties to collaborate on shared information at the same time. This reduces confusion and speeds up the verification processes. The shared nature of blockchains also strengthens storage effectiveness by not being able to be controlled by a single party and by eliminating any single faulty point that could more easily be exploited. Since Bitcoin began operating using a blockchain nine years ago in 2008, it has operated without a single technical flaw apparent in its design. All problems that have arisen have been contributed exclusively to malicious intentions through hacking or human error in management missteps.

Centralized networks present several points of vulnerability that can be exploited, in comparison to blockchain's decentralized network which avoids these weaknesses. At the basis of these networks are public and private keys. Keys are randomized strings of numbers used as "addresses" for designated users. A public key serves as a user's address on the blockchain and Bitcoins are recorded as being from that address. A private key acts more like a password to its user and used to gain access to data and recorded assets.

Transaction Fees. Fees are relative to how many bytes are in the transaction, rather than the Bitcoin amount. Simpler transactions are the cheapest to make, and transactions that follow a pattern of conventional activity will not pay unusually high fees. Most Bitcoin wallets automatically add what they feel is the fairest fee to transactions. Some transactions may be processed without fees, but these will take a much longer waiting periods (days to weeks). Transaction fees are used as protection against user manipulation against the network and as payment to miners securing the transaction network, as well as speeding up transactions, so they serve everyone involved.

The New Web and Blockchain Advantages. Blockchains are being referred to as the "new web" due to their solid answers to many of current networking's problems. Key features found in blockchains that seem promising for the future of the web include their ability to authenticate digital information through a virtually foolproof system, the implementation of placing power and opportunity into the hands of users, and an improved sharing economy building off of values previously utilized by successful technologies and apps such as transportation service Uber and middleman-lacking OpenBazaar (an app similar to eBay, without transaction fees or set rules). Identity management will be especially important in sharing economies – this is also offered an extra layer of protection by blockchain systems, making it easier for users to manage their online identities and prove who they are. Similarly, the cost of implementing policies that involve multi-step processes for a business to know who their new customers are could be drastically decreased while accuracy would increase.

Prediction markets may also find usefulness in prediction markets that payout according to event outcomes. Another of the current internet's major flaws are those that affect owners of copyrighted materials that lose certain rights and opportunities for income from their products. This can also be answered using blockchain technology to establish smart contracts and eliminate file redistribution and copying. These same smart contracts come in handy with the automation of remote systems. This system could also change the way the stock market works, via eliminating intermediaries and causing trade deals to become much quicker.

On a government-related scale, the transparency of blockchain systems presents the future possibility of truly public and honest elections and polls. The data distribution found in blockchains protects files from loss and hacking, in addition to speeding up file sharing and decluttering the current web's delivery systems – this would also potentially hasten streaming services such as Netflix and Internet-based music sharing apps. Another major advantage to utilizing the kind of web that could exist using blockchains is verification of claims made by companies concerning their products and practices via providing distributed ledgers. These public ledgers would display accurate payment amounts, dates, and locations – thus, for example, allowing a customer to verify a receipt or that a company's product was really made from within the United States.

CryptoNight. A proof of work algorithm, CryptoNight is designed to work exclusively on PC CPUs. CryptoNight works by randomly accessing slow memory and places emphasis of latency dependence. As in normal blockchain technology, in CryptoNight each new block depends on the establishment of the blocks before it.

Alternative Chain and Merged Mining. Using the blockchain algorithm, alternative chains aim to receive consensus on a specific topic. Miners of alternative chains may share a network with another platform, such as Bitcoin's. This is referred to as merged mining. Alternative chain systems are similar to blockchain in that they possess the capability to support unique elements in voting systems, peer to peer currency, timestamping, and file storage. While blockchain was created specifically for use with Bitcoin, the technology can be implemented in other networks and for other objectives.

Alternative chains can be created once what a transaction is within a unique network is defined. These transactions do not have to function in the same way Bitcoin transactions do. As Bitcoin and its innovative blockchain system grow in popularity and usage, as they have tended to over the last several years, the emergence of new ways to make money and mine different systems will most likely expand for miners, investors, traders, and other users to take advantage of.

Concerns. Criticisms against blockchain as well as Bitcoin concepts and technology include concerns about user privacy and too much control being placed into the hands of those controlling the apps. The idea of digital money that cannot exist outside of a computer is also a common concern of those more familiarized and comfortable regarding dealings with objects such as gold or natural resources. These concerns are comparable to the credit cards and online banking systems we already commonly use today. There are also concerns afoot of what may further develop from the concept of permanently tracking and monitoring every purchase and transaction a person makes, as well as theories that centralized government will one day take over and exploit the process and its users, while others gladly celebrate this guaranteed and non-negotiable honesty.

Virtually anyone can use specialized tools to process blockchain transactions via competing to complete mathematical puzzles in order to verify data, and as a result, earn Bitcoin rewards in exchange for the service - this is Bitcoin mining.

MATT COHEN

CHAPTER 3
MINING FOR PROFIT

At the heart of Bitcoin lies mining. Without miners, the network isn't as secure and doesn't truly work in the way it was designed to. Transaction fees are used to reward miners for the work they do and give an incentive to processing those transactions, building and verifying the blockchain, and securing the Bitcoin network.

In order to make a profit from Bitcoin mining, a sizable investment must, in most cases, first be made in the right hardware, software, and equipment. While it is technically possible for a new user to begin traditionally mining using only a personal computer, digital wallet (many of which are free), a mining program (many of which are also free), and internet connection, it will be virtually impossible for that user to find blocks in this way. It might be years before a user mines a single block.

Mining – sometimes referred to as *Proof of Work* – is the use of computer hardware power to secure transactions via solving complicated math problems in return for user compensation in digital currency, such as Bitcoins. Each block presented within the network has a math problem that a miner's computer must successfully solve in order for the block to be verified and added to the blockchain. Each time a block is mined, its transaction is verified.

Each block holds the potential reward of a set amount of digital coins that typically decreases over time. The network benefits from having many miners because the more miners are present mining blocks the more secure the network becomes. This also makes the Bitcoin more valuable and more difficult to obtain as more miners become present. The system makes an effort (via adjusting the difficulty of finding blocks) to ensure the average time it takes to find a block to mine remains equal to ten minutes, no matter how many people are mining at any present time.

In technical terms, during the mining process, your computer runs a cryptographic hashing function on a block header. The hash rate is the unit of the processing power of the Bitcoin network. For every new hash, the mining software will use a varied randomly generated number, or a nonce, on the header in a randomly generated order. Hashes appear as long sequences of numbers and letters and act as the backbone of mining systems. These are produced by miners typically at rates based on MH/s, megahashes per second. Other miners may produce hashes based on larger rates of hashes or megahashes per second.

It is worth remembering that the difficulty of mining will slightly increase the longer a user mines, and the profits made through Bitcoin mining have decreased over time as more users have joined the network as miners. Mining that used to make a person $170 per day a few years ago would now make that same person, using the same technology, roughly $30 a day, after factoring in electricity costs. As such, it's key to stay updated on software, hardware, and programs, and to have realistic goals for your Bitcoin profits. $30 a day, while it doesn't sound as impressive as $170 per day, does add up quick. A user could – for a while until the mining difficulty increased high enough to change these numbers – earn around $465 in a month if they were to consistently mine every single day of that month. Even with all of this information at a user's disposal, the price of Bitcoin fluctuates and is uncontrollable. Block price rewards, however, are somewhat predictable in that each block's value is halved every four years. Rewards previously were 50 Bitcoins per block – today, they are approximately 12.5 Bitcoins per block.

Another concern that arises with getting into Bitcoin mining is waiting for the arrival of ordered ASICs and other equipment. Production companies such as Butterfly Labs ran off of pre-orders some time ago, and people would receive their ordered products several months after the order was placed. The pre-order nature of such equipment is still very much in effect today. It is very likely that an order placed today will not arrive until later next year. Another problem with this, besides waiting such a long time to even get the hardware a user needs to begin mining, is the decrease in value in ASICs over time. What a user ordered today will not be worth in a year's time what it was worth when the order was placed.

One-way users get around this and cut down slightly on waiting times is by purchasing ASIC machines off of eBay. Sellers already on the waiting list for an ASIC machine will sell their place on the list to a buyer before they actually own the machine. The seller ships the item to the buyer as soon as the seller receives the item from the manufacturer.

Deciding if Bitcoin mining is profitable for an individual user or not comes down to a particular set of data. This data is not exclusive but can give potential miners a good idea if their hard work, efforts, time, and monetary investments are worthwhile. This set of data to consider is made up of the cost of an ASIC miner or another device, equipment costs to run the miner device, electricity usage costs, cost of a power supply unit or PSU, internet access fees, network gear costs, and the key value of Bitcoin during the duration of the miner's lifespan. Other subtle fees many miners can forget about include mining group fees should they be applicable, data center fees where applicable, and the costs of miscellaneous supportive gear such as cables, shelving, and storage for mining gear. It is important to note that internet access and electricity costs will be recurring fees when calculating a realistic profit. It is also worth acknowledging that profits for miners may generally decrease as the network's hash rates grow and difficulties raise.

99Bitcoins features a useful Bitcoin mining calculator on their website that can help users determine if they can really make a profit. This takes into account the difficulty factor of blocks to be mined, your device's hash rate, the block's Bitcoin reward, and the current exchange rate between Bitcoins and U.S. dollars. The calculator can be found online through this link: *https://99Bitcoins.com/Bitcoin-mining-calculator/*

Bitcoin Core and Running Full Nodes. These are programs that process and completely validate transactions and blocks. Full nodes accept blocks from each other to be verified, and then these blocks are sent on to other full nodes. Miners rely on these programs, and so will often run their own full nodes. In order to run a full node through Bitcoin Core or most other platforms, it is strongly encouraged to possess certain hardware requirements:

- A Computer running an updated, recent version of Windows, Linux, or Mac OS X, that you can keep running continually or for a minimum of six hours a day. Sleep or screensaver modes on this device should be disabled, and some anti-virus programs may make running Bitcoin Core more difficult or slow down the process
- 1-2 gigabytes of memory or RAM
- Minimal upload speed of 50 kilobytes per second on a broadband connection
- 145 gigabytes worth of free disk space
- An internet connection with high upload limits, capable of handling approximately 200-gigabyte uploads per month
- Capacity to download 500 megabytes per day, or 15 gigabytes per month

- Capacity of a 140-gigabyte one-time download the first time you start Bitcoin Core

It is important when running full nodes to be aware of your internet provider's conditions. Some providers may, without prior warning, disconnect internet usage due to overuse. Others may charge an additional fee for bandwidth uploads that are not included in your plan.

Hardware. Previously, almost anyone with a practical computer could begin mining. Now, as more miners have emerged, it has become increasingly difficult to mine blocks. Because of this, the only truly effective and profitable method of present-day mining is doing so with specialized hardware. Users can no longer make a profit from simply mining off of a normal laptop or desktop computer. The startup cost of purchasing mining hardware is often the most costly part of the entire processing. Purchasing the most efficient mining device on the market will cost an average of approximately $700 and mines blocks worth about $200 per month. This means it can really take a user nearly four months of mining just to earn back startup costs. This varies with the hardware purchased and what is currently available. The different hardware used for mining – in order from least effective to most effective – include CPUs, GPUs, FPGAs, and ASICs.

The least effective way to mine is through a CPU. CPU mining is sometimes referred to as the "golden age of mining" because it was the first and previously most common method. Today, only a few digital currencies can be mined using CPUs.

Bitcoin mining is done much more effectively with high-quality graphics cards. As such, GPUs allowed for a vast increase of power in mining when compared to previous hardware. GPUs are the most popular method for mining alternative online currencies. Gaming computers with advanced graphics cards are surprisingly great at acting as nodes and mining blocks. Radeon graphics cards tend to have a formidable edge over other popular graphics cards, such as powerful gaming graphics cards brand Nvidia when it comes to mining power.

FPGAs are simply the step up from GPUs to ASIC hardware in terms of mining power.

A Lancelot-A FPGA based bitcoin mining board

Mining with ASICs - Application Specific Integrated Circuits - is essentially the most powerful of the mining methods. The ASIC is a chip that exists only for the purpose of mining. These devices effectively aim to vastly improve hashing power (typically offering an increase by 100 times) and reduce energy consumption when compared to older technologies. While many alternative coins reject mining using ASICs, Bitcoin does accept it.

Th/s refers to a measuring unit for the hash rate, a user's terahashes or gigahashes (Gh/s) per second. Higher hash rates equate to more powerful mining capabilities. In addition to seeking out high hash rates for the most mining power, a miner's efficient use of energy is almost if not equally important. W/GH measures mining efficiency. The higher the W/GH, the less energy a device uses when mining.

Cooling fans are also necessary to include in a miner's setup when operating the kind of high electricity and heat producing work as Bitcoin mining. This being said, electric bill additions can be considered a monthly cost of mining and must be considered when calculating profit. Places with cheap electricity – such as China, Venezuela, or Washington State within the United States – are ideal for mining due to the increased profit. Another geological advantage many users may overlook are those miners who live in especially cold areas. People in these kinds of locations normally don't need to run cooling fans, and may even use their hardware to heat their homes during the coldest months. This ingenious method can be used to save money on a utility bill rather than increase costs, thus creating more of a profit.

Popular places to buy mining hardware include popular websites such as Amazon, eBay, and Newegg, and also Bitcoin mining hardware specific site BitMain.com. Wallet hardware can also be found on these sites, such as the positively reviewed Satoshi Labs Trezor wallet for $100. Naturally, a wide variety of fans, extension cords, and anything else you might need are also available on these websites. When buying hardware, it is important to do your research and buy the most updated, most compatible hardware only. Many old devices have become useless as Bitcoin mining difficulty and competition has risen.

Hardware Locations. Due to excessive heat produced by miner devices and computers using vast amounts of energy, most of the time these cannot be placed within most rooms of a home. Basements, garages, or other rooms that are not frequently inhabited by others who may be disturbed. These spaces must be able to handle the large amounts of heat put off and not pose any concerns due to noise production by the devices.
To avoid handling physical miners altogether, miners can use cloud mining services. Clouds do, however, come

with less security compared to using physical mining devices as well as decreased profits. Care and thorough research should be taken before registering for any cloud service. A few of the most reliable and top paying cloud mining websites as of this year are Bitcoin Pool, Hashnest, HashFlare (ETH), and Genesis Mining (ETH).

Software. The software used in mining plays hand in hand with the hardware used. There are several downloadable options to choose from with varying features to best suit many different miners.

- **BitMinter** focuses on ease of use and simple installation. The software belongs to a mining group and will require new users to fill out the signup form before being able to use the software. The registration form can be found here (you will need a current public key to sign up): *https://bitminter.com/login.*

- **CGminer** is the standard mining software for use with GPU, FPGA, and ASIC hardware. Its features include overclocking, fans control, monitoring options, self-detection of new blocks, GPU and CPU mining support, and remote capabilities. Download CGminer here: *https://github.com/ckolivas/cgminer.*

- **BFGminer** caters to FPGA and ASICs and is very similar to CGminer, without the GPU focused capabilities. If operating a ModMiner, ZTEK, or X6500 device along with BFGminer, users will need to download bitstreams found in the BFGminer forums (found here: *https://Bitcointalk.org/index.php?topic=168174.0*) and official website. BFGminer can be downloaded here: *https://github.com/luke-jr/bfgminer.*

- **Poclbm** is GPU mining software that allows users to perform hashing quickly and is known for being an excellent software used in mining experimentation and mining using multiple devices. Poclbm can be downloaded here: *https://github.com/m0mchil/poclbm*.

Block Difficulties. Difficulty Targeting is the process of making mining more challenging as more power and sources are entered into the network. As the difficulty increases, only the most advanced and powerful computers will be able to mine blocks. The mining difficulty is expressed in simple numbers that signify much bigger numbers (such as one trillion). Mining difficulty represents how much more challenging the present block will be to generate in comparison to the first block mined by the first miner. This difficulty system is implemented to maintain the average at which blocks are mined to ten minutes. As more users and hash power enter the network, there is more difficulty in mining. While there is no sure way to predict future difficulties, miners can follow technology trends to make educated estimates about the growth of network hash rates and block difficulty levels.

As of September 2017, the difficulty is recorded as 923233069449. The difficulty level (which is helpful to know when using the profit calculator included earlier in this chapter), as well as lots of other useful data and updates regarding Bitcoin and cryptocurrency, can be observed here at Bitcoincharts: *https://Bitcoincharts.com/*.

Due to Bitcoin nodes and the strict rules they automatically adhere to regarding invalid data, there is no possible way to cheat at Bitcoin mining or to process fraudulent transactions. This ensures the network is always safe, no matter miners' intentions.

Solitary or Group Mining. Mining can be done in solitary or within a mining group or pool. When mining alone, it can potentially take upwards of thousands of dollars to obtain hardware strong enough to successfully mine Bitcoin.
When miners work on a network together they combine

the power of each of their computers hash rates, thus becoming more successful and more profitable than those who choose to mine alone. Some of these groups require a fee while others are free to register for. Block rewards are typically split among participating members of the group, the member contributing the most power receiving the most profit. In comparison to group mining payouts which are smaller but more consistent, mining alone provides less frequent but larger payouts for a miner's work.

Alternative Mining Methods. In addition to traditional mining, there are alternatives that may prove more user-friendly or simple to utilize.

Proof of Stake mining, for example, doesn't require mining at all. In this method, the network is secured in that users have their wallets open, helping confirm pending transactions. Proof of Stake owners are awarded interest on all earned Bitcoins.

Proof of Burn mining involves sending or "burning" Bitcoins back to the blocks in which they came from. This is a popular method used within digital mining on Counterparty's systems.

Human Mining requires some sort of human-ran activity to mine, rather than putting the computer to work. The tasks involved are generally some type of game or something similar, in which coins are rewarded for the completed work. Huntercoin is known for incorporating this type of mining in an MMO-type computer game that rewards players with virtual currency, but there are a variety of other Bitcoin-using games, such as those involving slots, casino, poker, raffles, bingo, blackjack, or lotteries. A list of games involving Bitcoin earning potential can be found here: *https://en.Bitcoin.it/wiki/Category:Games*.

Pre-Mining is essentially what it sounds like. Block rewards on the first block are increased by developers and then blocks are mined before being publicly posted.

There is a negative stigma surrounding pre-mining. Instant Mining is mining that is not pre-mined, with the client publicly released to miners after developers have mined the coin. Developers have an advantage here in mining coins while users are still setting up.

Cloud Mining allows the user to delve into mining without spending large amounts of money or physical storage space on costly equipment but is not without its own cost. Many users find this method of mining to not yield much profit because of the fees charged by the providers. In this method, users rent their mining power from companies and receive payment according to how much power they own. Many cloud mining companies are in fact scams, but Genesis Mining *(https://www.genesis-mining.com/)* has been around for long enough to validate its authenticity as a reliable cloud mining company.

Cloud mining can be broken up into Hosted Mining and Buying Hashing Power. In hosted mining, the miner sends their mining device or a leased mining device to an electricity-providing firm. The firm takes care of not only electricity but also configurations and cooling needs. To protect the user against scams and malicious entities that are not authentic, miners should check that the cloud hosting provider is officially registered. Hosted mining presents a higher investment cost and a higher monthly cost than directly buying hash rate power. The monthly fee will depend upon how much energy is being used by the machine you bought. In addition, this mining method is also often somewhat more difficult to monitor compared to others. In buying hashing power, the miner does not need to actually own any mining device, computer, or mining software at all. There are no upkeep payments in this method, but scams do tend to be more abundant and generally harder to pinpoint than those spotted in hosted mining.

Known and publicly blacklisted scammers among cloud services, from the most recent dates, include HashOcean, Vulu, Burstmine, LTCGear, Mining Sweden, Bitcoin Cloud

Services, BitKnock, Scryptsy, CloudThink, CoinTracking, Scrypt.cc, xScrypt, and Cloudminr. These services have since been suspended, and users are advised to avoid them should they ever reopen in the future.

In addition to scams, there are also inactive cloud services that do not yield a profit and as such are not considered worth joining. These include OXBTC (MHS01), BitMiner, and Hashnest (S7).

Generally, cloud mining brings higher profits than other methods because hosts optimize everything to the fullest extent. This - and not needing to host any kind of miner device or equipment in a user's home - make this an appealing alternative to traditional mining. For those miners who don't want to be burdened with keeping up to date with updating technology and replacing mining devices, or configuring sometimes complex devices, this is a viable option.

Alternative Coins (Altcoins). Beyond Bitcoin, there are alternative digital currencies or Altcoins which tend to still be somewhat easier to mine in comparison. There are several Altcoins to choose from and caution must be executed no matter which you choose. Engaging in Altcoins should only be done following extensive research regarding each specific altcoin. The most highly recommended Altcoins are Dogecoin, Peercoin, and Litecoin.
In 2013, more Dogecoin transactions were processed than Bitcoin. This is especially impressive considering the currency's beginnings as a practical joke based off of the popular "doge" memes. Dogecoin's developers - like Bitcoin's - have emphasized that the currency's primary use is not for investing, but for transactions. One of Dogecoin's primary uses currently is online tipping between users, especially on websites such as Reddit. Unlike Bitcoin, 1 Dogecoin can be purchased for less than one cent.

Peercoin regulates its flow of coins more closely than Bitcoin and is designed to address the energy efficiency issues Bitcoin presents. It was designed with Bitcoin's current challenges and potential flaws in mind, aiming to answer these problems. It has not yet, however, come up to par with Bitcoin's huge network.

Litecoin is very similar to Bitcoin, but with easier mining and quicker transactions. Speed is a key feature of Litecoin. Mining can be done without the same expensive, impressive equipment Bitcoin demands, and there are more Litecoins available than Bitcoins.

Litecoin logo

Ecology and Energy. One Bitcoin transaction uses the same amount of electricity as nearly two average households' daily consumption. There are concerns about the vast amount of energy required to run mining devices and processes. Following trends, the further expansion of the Bitcoin network could up its energy consumption rates to that of the entire electricity consumption of Denmark by the year 2020. However, as mining is much more profitable and efficient in areas where electricity has low costs, some of these locations have low demand and high supply. It is a possibility that Bitcoin mining will only be profitable in these kinds of locations in the future.

In contrast to environmental costs, there are also benefits. Freeing up trade promotes economic growth while the impressive technological innovations coming along because of Bitcoin and its blockchain technology are worth mentioning. This poses the possibility of faster technological advancements occurring in response, perhaps ushering in a new age of tech and how it is used. Voting processes would become more trustworthy, cost-efficient, and verifiable if done using Bitcoin and blockchain networks. Environmentally destructive goods would also become much more transparent – consumers would be able to tell where a product was outsourced, and as a result be able to determine which products truly harmed or helped the environment. The entire process from point A to point B of how a particular product came into the hands of that consumer would be completely available.

CHAPTER 4
TRADING FOR PROFIT

While Bitcoin's value is volatile nature is a drawback for some users, for those looking to trade it can potentially bring a decent profit. Users who trade Bitcoins are buying the currency at a lower price than what they intend to sell it back for. Bitcoin is considered an asset with a value that is suggested, but not guaranteed, to rise over time. The trading market is not newcomer-friendly. To be successful in Bitcoin trading, the user must first have a solid understanding of what they are doing. Going into trading blindly leaves the user very susceptible to being taken advantage of by more experienced traders. There are several main factors to consider when purchasing Bitcoin to trade: the exchange rate based on a global price index, payment method preference and fees, how quickly a buyer needs the Bitcoins, buying limits differing from exchange site to exchange site, exchange service fees, privacy protection offered by specific payment methods and exchange sites, and the authenticity of an exchange site. It is safe practice to immediately after purchase transfer Bitcoins from exchange sites to Bitcoin wallets. Careful observation of the market is key for wise investment making. Etoro features a real-time Bitcoin price chart for U.S. dollars, including graphed stats, here: *https://www.etoro.com/markets/btc.*

While Bitcoin hasn't hit any major snags at this point in time, investors should consider any future possibilities that could cause the virtual market to crash. While currently not regulated by many jurisdictions, law enforcement is becoming increasingly interested in the network and the anonymity feature it possesses. Should laws be passed to remove the anonymity of users, Bitcoin would lose some of its appeal and the market would be likely to suffer. Another potential concern to consider is that of system failure of the Bitcoin computer network.

Many users find the best profit outcome to come from selling Bitcoins on website LocalbitCoins. The service offers private buying which attracts buyers willing to pay extra in exchange for the privacy of their buying habits. Selling in person is the other method that tends to yield the best payouts but requires a bit more effort than online buying methods. As an advantage, LocalbitCoins contains profiles for each of its users' history and reviews, allowing users to seek out buyers with the best feedback.

BTC-E.com is one of the more popular, easiest to get into exchanges for users to begin trading Bitcoins. The company relies on an operation process where the due money is transferred between several banks and processors before being deposited. Because of this complex transaction process, BTC-E poses a risk of losing money between transactions. To get around this, most BTC-E users utilize deposit and withdrawal features that support several digital wallets such as Perfect Money and E-Money, as well as PayPal.

Trading Platforms. It's important to only make Bitcoin trades on trusted, reputable websites. Investors and traders must do their own research carefully and make their own decisions about when and where to trade their Bitcoins.
Derivative Markets. Derivatives are contracts that base their value on an upcoming future asset. Bitcoin derivative markets allow users to buy and sell "Bitcoin

futures contracts" regarding which way the user believes the market will go. These allow users to make a profit, regardless of the increase or decrease in Bitcoin value. This can be a helpful asset, given the nature of Bitcoin's ever-changing value spikes and waves.

Derivative markets involve either long or short positions. In a long position, the user borrows cash or other fiat currency in order to purchase Bitcoins. This is done with the hopes of selling those Bitcoins at a higher price. In a short position, the user borrows Bitcoins to sell for cash or other fiat currency. This is done with the goal of buying Bitcoins in return at a lower price.

Margin Trading. Peer-to-peer (P2P) funding providers allow users to trade Bitcoins at a funding fee. Such as in derivative markets, margin trading involves either long or short positions, as well as the addition of either daily or term funding fee payment, or margin funding type. In daily funding, the margin funding fees a user has accumulated will be withdrawn from the user's wallet used in trading each day. These wallets cannot be used to buy or sell Bitcoins, only to trade via margin trading systems. In term funding, margin funding fees will accumulate into the funding balance of a user's position until the user closes this position. Positions may be closed at any time without penalty. When a position is closed, the lender is reimbursed and the position is credited as either a loss or a profit. Positions cannot be opened if there is no margin funding provider presently available.

Faucets and Jobs. A considerable option for those who want to get their first few Bitcoins to start trading without having to buy them, Bitcoin faucets are websites that give out tiny amounts over several minutes. After a user enters their Bitcoin address and solves a captcha, they can hit a confirmation button and receive a random number of Bitcoins from the site. Most faucets come with a set of particular rules, such as that a user can only claim Bitcoins once every five minutes and bots will not be tolerated.

Registration form for joining 99Bitcoins' faucet page to earn a few coins, as a good place to start, can be found here: *https://99Bitcoins.com/wishlist-member/?reg=1477123177* and a complete set of this particular faucet's rules and guidelines can be found here: *https://99Bitcoins.com/Bitcoin-faucet-rules/*.

Faucet rotators are websites that combine many different faucets from other sites. The primary advantage to these is that they make the process of finding and using faucets go much more smoothly, but it should be understood that they will not make anyone rich.

Alternatively, there are other ways to earn Bitcoins, either simply on the side or as a beginning amount to experiment with in trading and the market. There are several jobs – many of which posted in the Reddit work board, here: *https://www.reddit.com/r/Jobs4Bitcoins/* – that reward workers in Bitcoins. These jobs range from everything between graphic design, helping other users set up their mining equipment and review writing, to website review and serving as a virtual assistant.

In order to ensure protection when engaging in these job agreements, there are several security precautions users should take and due diligence must be executed here. Using an escrow is suggested, as well as checking the posting history of any job posters.

CHAPTER 5
INVESTING IN BITCOIN

Investors have compared Bitcoin's market and numbers to the 1920s stock market boom, the 2000s housing boom, and 1990s technology boom. Some argue that this boom has reached its peak and the days of making money with Bitcoin are over, while other argue Bitcoin is the most promising investment today. Many are skeptical of this market crashing and burning, while others are excitedly confident that Bitcoin is *the* big thing right now and should not be underestimated by any means, and others believe investing in *other* up-and-coming cryptocurrencies is the best move at this point and will produce similar results to those who invested in Bitcoin several years ago and are now in possession of an impressive fortune, some of these early investors even millionaires.

Investing in Bitcoin is unique in that it is not a stock or company, but a currency. This means when someone invests in Bitcoin, they are buying currency. As is the case with investing in virtually anything, a sense of entrepreneurship must be executed when deciding to invest in Bitcoin. Efforts to invest will be competitive, somewhat unpredictable, and will always hold risk. Though Bitcoin has continued to grow at an exceptionally fast rate, there is no promise that it will continue to do so, and its currency's value is in fact often still fluctuating, due in part to its lack of large-scale acceptance and awareness. At this time, Bitcoin is seen as a high-risk asset with an unpredictable economy. Saving anything you cannot afford to lose in Bitcoin is, of course, understandably discouraged by most websites, developers, exchanges, and all those involved in the community. Luckily, Bitcoin can be converted to local currencies (such as U.S. dollars) relatively easily by certain service providers.

Bitcoin value is determined, like most things, by fluctuating supply-and-demand waves. Because the Bitcoin market is still relatively small, even rather minor amounts of money potentially possess the ability to shift the market price. However reliable Bitcoin has been proven to be over the last several years, it is always possible for a currency to fail and become obsolete. In the past, currencies becoming worthless was typically due to hyperinflation – this, by the system's design, theoretically cannot exist within Bitcoin. However, there is still chance for Bitcoin to be overpowered by competing currencies, system and technical failures to occur, the arising of political problems to interfere or the onset of other events that could ultimately make Bitcoin worthless. No currency should ever be considered absolutely safe, and Bitcoin – however promising – is no exception.

The most common form of investing in Bitcoin is purchasing and holding onto the currency. Investors who engage in this belief, or at least hope, that the value of Bitcoin will rise over time. Whether or not the value will rise is anyone's guess. No one can accurately predict the future of Bitcoin, and so investors must trust their own intuition regarding the currency's trends over time and when the best time to buy maybe.

What Drives Prices. Government regulation is one of the main driving factors behind the price of Bitcoins. Many investors observe government policies and debates to get a sense of how this factor may change over time.

No one can with complete certainty predict how these trends will go, and so it is up to each individual investor to decide what they believe will happen next and when the best time to invest – or avoid investing – will be.

Other indicators of the value of Bitcoin and how it might move include political factors and world events, updates to laws especially those regarding cryptocurrency exchanges, and changes to Bitcoin's policies and network. The more informed an investor is of all of these things, the more of an advantage they may have.

Correlations. Assets can be divided, generally, into three categories; capital assets, consumable transformable assets, and store of value assets. Capital assets are those that are capable of generating future profit, thus are sensitive to change in the discount rate. Consumable transformable assets are things like physical commodities, those that in themselves cannot bring future profit but can be transferred into other assets. The asset's supply and demand quality is most important in this case. The store of value assets don't generate income and cannot be consumed, and yet they hold economic value. These assets are only worth something because people have attributed value to it, such as collectibles and currencies. Bitcoin is categorized as a store of value asset and thus is related to similar assets such as gold, the U.S. dollar, Swiss franc, and Japanese yen. However, the correlation between Bitcoin and these is extremely low. In fact, that are few other assets that hold such little correlation like this, hinting that Bitcoin is unaffected by macroeconomic factors, unlike most other assets. This is considered unusual. It also suggests that Bitcoin is unaffected, by design, by negative geopolitical risks.
This is supported by the recent Bitcoin price increase – an 80% increase in 2016 – following UK voters exiting the European Union, the compromise of Bitcoin exchange Bitfinex, the halving of Bitcoin mining rewards per block, and thus the reduction of new Bitcoins generated per each transaction (from 25 to 12.5 Bitcoins). The Bitfinex hacking lost about 120,000 Bitcoins and the exchange stopped trading for a short time. During this time, Bitcoin

prices dropped 20% but recovered in the next few days. When Trump won the presidency, the stock market faced a general decline. Bitcoin, however, increased in prices and continued an upward trajectory.

Circulation Concerns and Deflationary Spiral Theory. According to this economic theory, if there is an expectation for prices to drop, users will postpone purchases in order to reap lower prices. The fall in demand will cause merchants to lower prices to meet demands, causing a spiraling problem and ultimately leading to a depression. This controversial theory has been brought up in the past as a concern with Bitcoin's economy, but its concept has not consistently been proven true in actual scenarios. One example where this theory fails is that of consumer electronics. One way in which Bitcoin circulation may suffer severely is if many users lost their digital wallets and a large amount of money essentially vanished in this way.

High Yield Investment Programs and Scams. Any website or app claiming to "double your Bitcoins" or pay a hefty sum for daily interest on a user's earnings is generally, a scam. Programs like these promise to double money paid to them as start-up fees, use other start-up fees to begin owning up to their previous promises in order to create a good name for themselves around the web, incorporate referral programs to attract additional new users to bring in more money, and then suddenly go offline in a few months. The promised money is nowhere to be found and the money users spent on the program is now lost.

Bitcoin has been denounced by some as nothing more than a Ponzi scheme – a fraudulent investment that is based on a nonexistent enterprise promising quick returns to the initial investors by the newer investors. This theory is supported for some by the anonymity of the Bitcoin creator, whose identity is still not certain. However, others recognize that this anonymity is s good face for the decentralized network and stays true to Bitcoin's values and ideas.

99Bitcoins, in addition to their mining profit calculator previously included as a helpful resource, features a Bitcoin Scam Test on their website. The objective of the test is to determine if a website or service is legitimate or a scam, complete with sidebar tools to help with any questions a user may have difficulty answering within the test. Some of these tools can be helpful on their own, such as domain authority checkers, quick access to reviews, and registration checkers. This test and the accompanying sidebar tools can be found here: *https://99Bitcoins.com/Bitcoin-scam-test/*.

Dollar Cost Averaging. Rather than buying a large amount of Bitcoins in one exchange, dollar cost averaging involves buying a smaller fixed amount at a set time on a schedule (daily, weekly, or monthly) over the course of a year. Using this technique, investors purchase more shares with low prices and less when prices are high. While this technique does not promise the investor won't suffer losses rather than gains, it does spread investments over time rather than an investment being a lump sum. Some advantages to this method include not needing to focus on investing at top of the market or exiting or entering the investment market.

Hedge Strategy. Hedging takes advantage of the behavior of Bitcoin prices and involves selling Bitcoins in order to reduce the risks that come with holding them. This should, in theory, increase profits. When the price of Bitcoin raises, users hold their coins. When users believe the price is about to drop, they sell their Bitcoins at the highest price they can manage. Hints for these kinds of predictions can be found by checking the Bitcoin price range updated live on website Coindesk, found here: *https://www.coindesk.com/*. Other resources to help investors make decisions might include paying attention to news articles. Policy changes and legal updates are things to watch out for. Another helpful resource to check is CoinCheckup, which gives in-depth analysis of trends, predictions, investments, and the market. It can be found here: *https://coincheckup.com/*.

Users who hedge Bitcoins are, ideally, always growing their account and do not need to continually deposit coins or make impulsive investments. It is generally considered less risky than margin trading and other similar methods. While the principles are simple, most people who find success from hedging are experienced Bitcoin investors. Kraken is the most widely recommended platform for this method due to its speed, high limits, and convenience.

CHAPTER 6
BITCOIN WALLETS AND SECURING YOUR COIN

Choosing storage methods and wallet types is the primary step to securing Bitcoins. Without secure storage, Bitcoin earning can be made entirely in vain. As with dealing with any kind of valuable asset or money, Bitcoins should be treated very carefully and with some degree of precaution and thought as to storage, especially when dealing with larger sums. There are advantages and disadvantages to every wallet and storage type. Use of several wallets and many different storage techniques are recommended.

Wallets are virtual bank accounts used to store Bitcoins on a user's computer, or other device,s or within a cloud. These wallets generate public and private keys and allow users to send or receive payments. Unlike a standard bank account, digital wallets are not insured by the FDIC, which poses some risk for users. In addition, wallets held on cloud servers may be hacked or companies may vanish with their clients' Bitcoins, and wallets held on personal computers can easily be accidentally deleted or destroyed by viruses. Digital wallets should be treated somewhat like normal wallets in that you should only store everyday spending money in them, not impressive amounts. Should a user's digital wallet ever be lost, the money within it goes permanently out of circulation, unable to be redeemed by any user without the private key(s). While unusable, this amount remains recorded in the blockchain.

Private keys, or seeds, are pieces of secret data stashed within Bitcoin wallets and used to sign transactions. Typically, these begin with a "5" and are a sequence of 51 alphanumeric characters. These keys provide proof that the owner of the wallet is the one making each transaction and use mathematical assessments to protect the transaction from being altered or interfered with. Keeping all Bitcoin and wallet software currently updated is also important to take advantage of all new security upgrades and system improvements.

Wallet Types. Understanding the different wallets available to you and assuring you are using safe, secure storage methods is of utmost importance when handling Bitcoins. You may choose to only use one very secure and trusted wallet or to disperse your coins across several platforms. Depositing your Bitcoins between several wallets is usually the best bet for security and protection against loss or theft, especially when dealing with larger amounts. It is important to note that digital wallets are not yet as powerful as banks, and may be susceptible to vulnerabilities and exploitation.

Paper wallets are physical records of private and public keys, such as receipts printed by the previously mentioned Bitcoin ATMs. These hand-written records store Bitcoin in a physical format. Alternatively, paper wallet generator software is available for written digital storage. This, however, does still pose the risk of vulnerability to hacker spyware. Paper wallets are best used by users who make few transactions of a high value, or those with a large amount of Bitcoins that they do not need to use or relocate frequently. It is usually best for the user to create their own paper wallet rather than use an online service.

Mobile wallets are those such as Bitcoin Wallet. These

provide plenty of flexibility and ease of accessibility, and transactions can be made via QR code scanning through these wallets. They are best used by those consumers who use Bitcoin mainly to buy small items or many otherwise low-value transactions. Most modern smartphones with up-to-date software are sufficiently secure.

Desktop wallets include those such as Bitcoin Core and are installed on your computer. This gives the user complete control over their digital wallet. As such, it is the user's responsibility to create backups and properly protect their wallet.

Web-based wallets provide the most flexibility and accessibility, as well as the most risk. Your Bitcoins are hosted by these wallets, and so choosing only the most trusted and secure web-based wallet is crucial for safe Bitcoin storage. Users who make few transactions of low value will benefit most from this option. Strong passwords are a must as these wallets can be accessed from any device, not just the one you created the wallet on.

Hardware wallets are especially suggested if the user has a large amount of money in their Bitcoin savings, namely those users who conduct a business that uses Bitcoins. These resemble USB flash drives and store private keys on a specialized chip. These wallets are unaffected if your phone or computer is compromised. Theft or loss is also of little harm because the wallets are password protected. This is the only wallet option that will cost the user money to purchase, running an average of $100.

Desktop Wallets

- **Electrum** is the most popular desktop wallet today. It is lightweight and encrypted but has an outdated looking and unfriendly user interface that turns many users off.

- **Exodus** is much more user-friendly than the above option as well as more aesthetically pleasing. This is a good option for Bitcoin beginners due to its simplicity of use.

- **Bitcoin Core** is the original heavy-duty digital wallet and offers good security to its users. It comes with the full blockchain and requires a lot of free computer space, approximately 130 gigabytes, and is designed for use by more experienced Bitcoin users. It does run slower than other desktop wallet options.

- **Armory** is a well-established wallet that offers cold storage and multi-signature authentication, offering great protection for desktop users. Known for its advanced security options and multiple layers of protection, it is best suited for more experienced Bitcoin users.

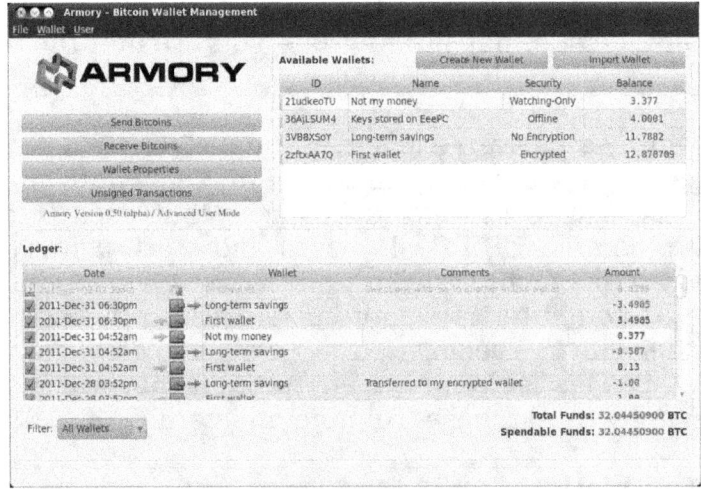

The user interface of Armory running on Ubuntu Linux

- **Copay** is a multi-signature wallet for enhanced security, and as such is a good option for those who cannot afford a hardware wallet.

Mobile Wallet Apps, for Android and iOS

- **Mycelium** is the top recommended digital wallet app for mobile devices. Top-notch security and private key deletion features are just some of the benefits to this app.

- **Wirex** offers great accessibility while upholding quality security measures. It can be accessed from desktop or mobile device.

- **Xapo** is known for its security, enforced by cold storage and multi-signature features.

Web-Based Wallets

- **Blockchain.info** is the standard website wallet for those that choose to use one. User-friendly and well-known, Blockchain.info provides support for multiple countries and can also be downloaded as a mobile or desktop application.

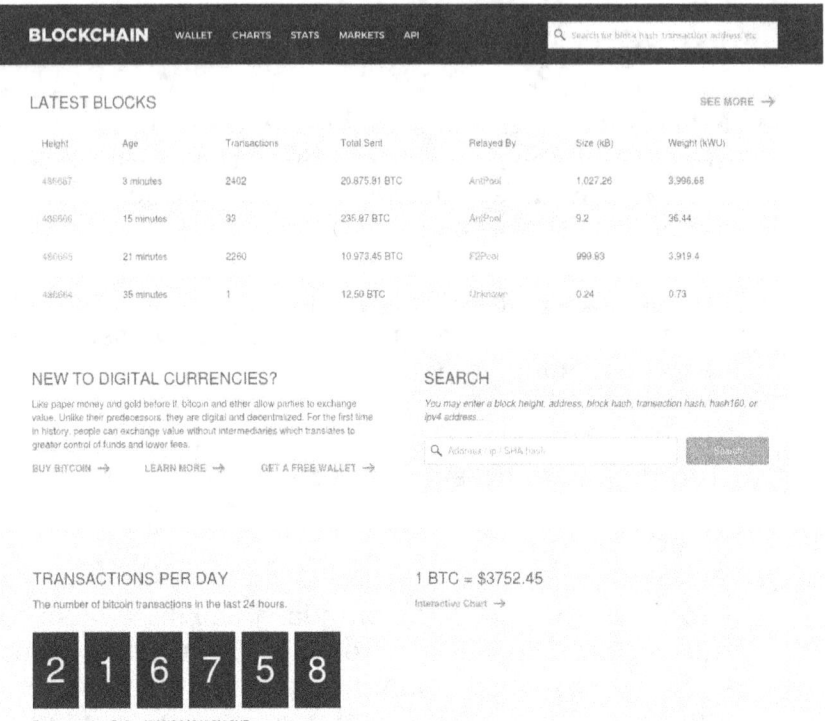

Blockchain.info

- **BitGo** is praised for its especially fast Bitcoin transactions.

- **GreenAddress** provides a watch-only mode for users who like to check their Bitcoin balance frequently without the security compromise presented by frequently entering and re-entering login info.

Hardware Wallets

- **KeepKey** enables an extra layer of protection for its users via requiring manual approvals through the device for each outgoing transaction. In case of loss or theft, the device is also PIN-protected.

- **Trezor** is a compact device with anti-malware security and recovery options.

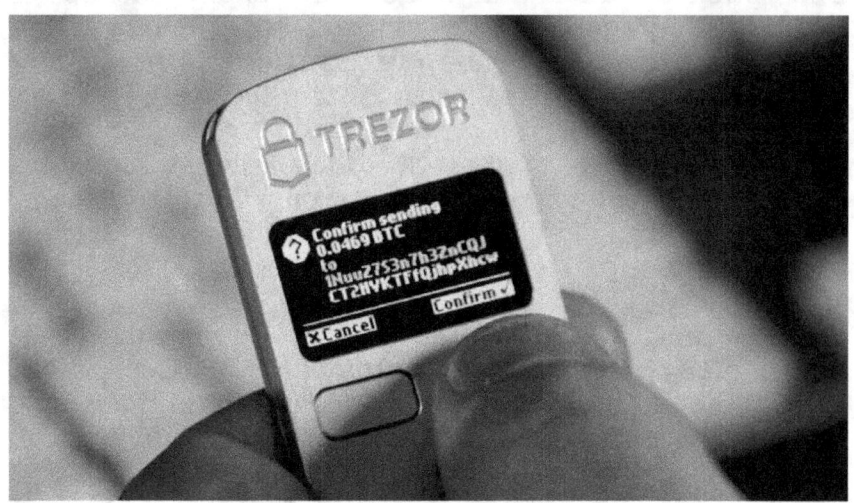

Confirming a transaction on Trezor Hardware Wallet

- **Ledger Nano** is the least expensive hardware wallet option, as well as one of its builds (Ledger Nano S.) being the first wallet capable of storing Ether.

Paper Wallets

- **Bitcoin Paper Wallet** allows users to print offline paper wallets. The website offers tips and additional security features and is the most popular cold storage website.

- **BitAddress** is especially user-friendly and completely free: *www.BitAddress.org*

Backups and Safe Storage. Backing up your Bitcoin wallet can come in handy when human errors, stealing, or computer malfunctions occur. It is ideal to keep wallet backups in several different places, such as on USB flash drives, within external hard-drives, on CDs, written on paper, and so on. Online backups are especially susceptible to theft and malicious viruses or software. Encryption for all digital wallets and online backups is highly encouraged. It is important to remember that backing up only the visible private keys will not secure your wallet, as many wallets use internal private keys

Offline wallets, also referred to as cold storage, are perhaps the safest storage for your Bitcoin savings. There are two primary methods for offline wallet storage, offline transaction storage and hardware wallets.

Offline transaction storage involves sharing a wallet between two computers. One computer is disconnected from all networks. This is the only computer in the pair to hold the wallet in its entirety or to be able to sign transactions. The other computer is connected to a network and only holds a wallet that is capable of creating unsigned transactions. In order to securely create a new transaction using this method, the new transaction is created on the online computer and saved on a USB drive. It is then signed with the offline computer, and then the signed transaction is sent via the online computer.

Hardware wallets are devices designed for the specific purpose of acting as a wallet for the digital currency. These hardware devices cannot have a software installed on them and many offer backup and recovery for your funds, even if you lose the device.
In addition, Bitcoin and some online wallets offer a multi-signature feature that can be utilized for the best anti-fraud protection. This feature requires a transaction receive signatures from multiple private keys before a withdrawal or other transaction can be accepted.

Sweeping versus Importing Private Keys. Sweeping sends Bitcoins to a new address controlled by a new private key. Importing is simply allows a user to access their Bitcoins in one location – such as, for example, a paper receipt printed by a Bitcoin ATM. Imported Bitcoins are still controlled by the original private key they were under. The sweeping process will differ between which wallet app is used. It is important to understand the difference between sweeping and importing whenever dealing with the relocation of Bitcoins.

Escrow Protection. Bitcoin transactions are designed with a relatively high layer of protection at the foundation. These transactions are irreversible and cannot be altered. However, extra protection can be added in the form of third-party escrow services. These services handle Bitcoin payments and provide a sense of security when buying from a party that is not well-established or not completely trusted. Escrow requires Bitcoins be deposited upfront and protects the buyer if the sale does turn out to be a scam or fail to deliver.

However, there are not many well-established escrow services currently operating today, which returns to the same issue of distrust and potential fraud that escrow users are already trying to solve. Even long-standing escrow providers tend to have mixed reviews from users, and many of these services end up being discontinued and their websites taken down within a few months' time.

Escrow protection can be categorized into four common types: regular escrow, regular escrow pegged to fiat value (dollar value), multi-signature escrow, and multi-signature escrow pegged to a fiat value.

In regular escrow, funds are first deposited into a site-owned Bitcoin address and then moved to a cold storage unit. Regular escrow pegged to a fiat value involves depositing Bitcoins into an address and then the value of those Bitcoins is pegged to a fiat value. Multi-signature escrow and multi-signature escrow pegged to a fiat value entail what they sound like.

DO
- Store your earnings in your own Bitcoin wallet(s).
- Store Bitcoins in multiple secure areas, such as an

offline computer, an external drive, a paper "wallet" including your private keys, multiple digital wallets, etc.
- Research wallets, clouds, and other storage units thoroughly.
- Consider how your heirs may access any Bitcoins you leave behind in the event of your death.
- Keep your private keys private and secure.

DON'T
- Store all or any of your Bitcoins in an exchange's wallet. This gives the third-party full access to your money.
- Keep all of your Bitcoins in one place.
- Trust any wallet, cloud, or application blindly without thorough research.
- Invest in alternative coins other than Bitcoin without first doing your research. Make sure if you do invest in other virtual coins that they are not a fraud or else simply a bad investment, as several are just that.
- Share your private keys with anyone.

CONCLUSION

Thank for making it through to the end of this book, let's hope it was informative and able to provide you with all of the tools you need to achieve your goals whatever they may be. Bitcoin can be a difficult concept for anyone to comprehend, especially for those not well versed in technology and the concept of cryptocurrency. The detailed explanations were hopefully useful in explaining the many different workings of Bitcoin and its connected elements, such as the innovation of blockchain technology.

Bitcoin is not a "get rich quick" ordeal, but can provide you with substantial profits if the proper amount of time, effort, and research is put in.

The next step is to put the information in this book to good use in your Bitcoin mining, trading, and investing endeavors. Now might be a good time to think about when the best time to invest will be based on what you now know, establish enhanced security through your wallets strategy, and explore some of the websites, apps, resources, and tools found in this book. Successful Bitcoin investments, trading, and mining must be executed with diligence, caution, and intuition. The benefits and excitement that can be found within Bitcoin make the risks well worth it to many users. No matter your goals going into the world of virtual currencies or delving deeper, this book aims to remain a resourceful guide along the way.

Finally, if you found this book useful in any way, a review on Amazon is always appreciated!

www.ingramcontent.com/pod-product-compliance
Lightning Source LLC
Chambersburg PA
CBHW050016230526
45470CB00003B/989